On your mark,
get set,
RELAX.

That's the key to winning at sports or to just plain feeling good, and the STRETCH OUT program will show you how. With a simple set of exercises you can do every day, use as a warm-up for your favorite sport, or use as a foolproof prescription for relief from tension and stress.

The STRETCH OUT program will make you look better, play better, and feel great.

Stretch Out

Warm Up and Beat Stress

by Stephanie Sorine
photographs by Daniel S. Sorine

Prince Paperbacks
Crown Publishers, Inc.
New York

Acknowledgments

Special thanks to Helene Alexopoulos and
Ulrik Trojaborg for demonstrating these
stretches.

Publisher's Note: This book includes exercise instructions
and exercise programs for the reader to follow. However,
not all exercises are designed for all individuals. Before
starting these or any other exercises or exercise program
you should consult your doctor for advice.

A Prince Paperback Book
Published by Crown Publishers, Inc., One Park Avenue,
New York, New York 10016, and simultaneously in Canada
by General Publishing Company Limited
Prince Paperbacks and colophon are trademarks of Crown
Publishers, Inc.
Manufactured in the United States of America

Library of Congress Cataloging in Publication Data
Sorine, Stephanie Riva.
    Stretch out.
    (Prince paperbacks)
    1. Exercise.   2. Stretch (Physiology).   I. Title.
GV481.S645   1984   613.7'1   84-7823
ISBN 0-517-55476-3 (pbk.)
10 9 8 7 6 5 4 3 2 1
First Edition

Contents

Introduction

Stretching is the most natural, painless, and reliable method of toning and limbering up muscles, loosening stiff joints, warming up for whatever is to follow, and cooling down afterward. It is a proven way to increase your achievement and performance in any physical activity, including aerobic dance, aerobic workout, weight training, running, tennis, golf, skiing, training on fitness machines, and swimming.

Stretching is a must for any fitness program. It is essential to stretch if you want to keep your body young, agile, and pain-free at any age.

This is a complete stretching program I designed for men and women of all ages and at all fitness levels. It has the Stretch Out, a workout of basic stretches that concentrates on different areas of the body in a prescribed order to gradually stretch every part of you; Stretches with Extras, a series of stretches using a chair or bench, ledge, wall, tree, or whatever else provides support; Spontaneous Stretching, some recommended stretches for everyday and anywhere use; and Taking 5, specific stretches combined as warm-ups and cool-downs for various sports and other physical activities.

Warming up, stretching out, and cooling down as you do in the Stretch Out, in addition to the other stretches described in this book, will make you more flexible very quickly. After only a week, you'll notice improvements in your muscular and joint mobility. Within a few months, you'll achieve nearly all of your maximum flexibility.

The Stretch Out program will also:

• Enhance your muscle tone, enabling you to avoid injuries and lower-back pain by relaxing and elongating your muscles.

• Prevent the soreness and stiffness associated with getting older, by releasing tension and improving joint mobility.

• Help you perform at your utmost by boosting the efficiency of each movement.

Healthier posture; less stress; better circulation and moods; more grace, energy, and coordination; a leaner, firmer body; and a clearer mind are just a few of the other benefits you'll soon experience, which will instantly improve the quality of your life.

Instead of ballistic stretches, in which you bounce and move to increase the stretch, these are static stretches: hold-and-stretch exercises. They are based on the simultaneous contraction and relaxation of the muscle groups. While you hold a stretch and focus on stretching that muscle group by lengthening and relaxing it, you are also strengthening the opposite group of muscles by contracting it. For example, when you stretch the back of your legs (your hamstrings), you strengthen the front of your legs (your quadriceps) at the same time.

Naturally, you'll be more flexible in one or more places, tighter in others. So some stretches will seem easier to do than others. Aging, stress, some occupations, aerobics, workouts, running, some other exercise, and sports, and, of course, inactivity can often actually tighten and shorten muscles, leading to a stiff, ungraceful body. Physical structure, and excess body fat are other factors that may also limit your flexibility and your possible range of motion.

But no matter how limber you are or what you do, in the Stretch Out program you stretch according to your own level of flexibility, reaching for your own goals.

Each exercise is preceded by a list of those areas being stretched—the body parts that are stretched the most coming first, followed after a slash (/), by those deriving secondary benefits—so if you like, you can modify this program to work on your tightest and stiffest areas. You can emphasize leg and back flexibility, or zero in on stretching your calves or waist, or get rid of the tension around your neck and shoulders simply to feel more at ease.

Through this program, I try to encourage you to do what's most important about stretching: *doing it regularly and doing it right.*

Here's why: not stretching at all, stretching incorrectly, or even stretching too strenuously can do much more harm than good. That's the main reason so many people get hurt from their workouts, runs, etc., and why they're not as flexible or fit as they could be, or stay as young in looks and spirit.

Stretching is both pleasurable and highly effective, which is why the Stretch Out program feels as good to you as it is for you.

To your health and happiness . . .

Getting Ready to Start

To help you get the most out of this book and achieve optimum results, here are a few guidelines and stretching tips.

- Anyone can stretch, but people differ in their capabilities. Before you start this or any exercise program, it's a good idea to get your physician's approval.

- Wear something comfortable that allows you to move freely.

- You may want to use a towel, rug, or mat for those exercises done sitting, lying down, or on your knees.

- Do these exercises any time of day, wherever you are—at least three times a week: before and after other activities such as aerobics, working out, training on fitness machines, running, or engaging in sports, as your warm-up and cool-down. Alternate days of your more physical activities with the Stretch Out. It's wise to do a lighter exercise session the day after a strenuous one. This allows your muscles time to recover and helps prevent soreness and injury.

- Do Stretches with Extras, Spontaneous Stretching, and Taking 5 as often as necessary and whenever you like.

- Do each exercise slowly and deliberately. Precision rather than speed should be your goal.

- While you do these exercises, keep your abdominal muscles pulled in tight toward your back, to firm, flatten, and strengthen them.

- Your own body weight should provide enough resistance during these stretches, but if you are an advanced exerciser or become used to these exercises and want more of a

4

challenge, when it is practical, do the arm, chest, and shoulder stretches with wrist or hand-held weights and the leg stretches with ankle weights. Weights of one to five pounds are recommended.

- For the first few seconds of the stretch, just ease into position. Never force anything. Focus your attention on those parts of your body being stretched.

- After you've held the stretch for a few seconds, stretch a little farther, but never strain a stretch. Let your muscles lengthen at their own pace.

- Concentrate on relaxing your muscles. Close your eyes, if you wish. The more you relax, the farther you'll be able to stretch.

- Don't bounce. Remember, these are static stretches, not ballistic ones. The idea here is to relax muscles, not tense them up and cause them to go into spasm, tighten, and possibly tear or pull.

- Never hold your breath. Keep your breathing steady.

- In the last seconds of the stretch, try to reach your maximum stretch, then relax into that. But don't overstretch. The tension in the stretch should decrease during this last stage; if not, you're overstretching.

- Finally, after you've held the stretch the suggested seconds, reverse the movements you used to get into the stretch—gradually, slowly, with control.

- When you feel ready, follow my instructions to advance these stretches.

- Along with this program, get aerobic exercise through activities such as fast walking, running, bicycling, playing racket sports, jumping rope, swimming, aerobic dancing, and cross-country skiing. And do some strength-building exercises, such as calisthenics and weight training, for a totally balanced fitness program.

The Stretch Out

WARMING UP 7-10 minutes

1

Cardiovascular System

- Since your body stretches more easily when the cardiovascular system has been warmed up, the Stretch Out starts with this aerobic exercise to stimulate the flow of blood to your muslces.

- Stand straight. Jog in place, barely lifting your feet off the floor, for 2 minutes.

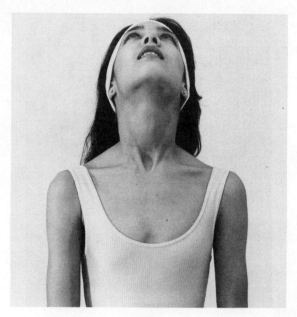

2

Neck

- Stand with your feet shoulder-width apart, arms at your sides, for these head circles.

- Inhale. Exhale as you tilt your head over your right shoulder. Hold and stretch for 2 seconds.

- Inhale. Exhale as you rotate your head back. Hold and stretch for 2 seconds.

- Continue the circle. Inhale. Exhale as you tilt your head over your left shoulder. Hold and stretch for 2 seconds.

- Inhale. Exhale as you lower your chin to your chest. Hold and stretch for 2 seconds.

- Reverse the circle. Repeat 2 times.

Advance by holding and stretching for 5 seconds in each position and taking deeper breaths.

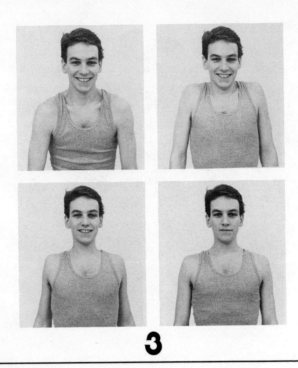

3

Shoulders

- Stand with your arms at your sides for these shoulder circles.

- Inhale. Exhale as you pull your shoulders forward. Hold and stretch for 2 seconds.

- Inhale. Exhale as you lift your shoulder up toward your ears. Hold and stretch for 2 seconds.

- Inhale. Exhale as you pull your shoulders back. Hold and stretch for 2 seconds.

- Inhale. Exhale as you press your shoulders down. Hold and stretch for 2 seconds.

- Reverse the circle. Repeat 2 times.

Advance by holding and stretching for 5 seconds in each position and taking deeper breaths.

4

Arms • *Shoulders*
- Stand straight. Raise your right arm overhead. Put your left arm down at your side.

- Inhale. Exhale as you reach your right hand up to the ceiling and your left arm down to the floor. Hold and stretch for 15 seconds, breathing freely.

- Do the same with the opposite arms. Repeat 2 times.

Advance by holding and stretching for 25 seconds.

5

Chest, Shoulders • *Arms*

• Standing tall, hold a towel between your hands behind your back.

• Inhale. Exhale as you lift your arms up. Don't hunch your shoulders. Hold and stretch for 10 seconds, breathing freely.

• Lower your arms. Repeat 4 times.

Advance by holding the stretching for 15 seconds, placing your hands closer together on the towel, or interlacing your fingers behind your back with elbows straight.

6

Waist, Chest • *Arms, Shoulders*

- Stand with your feet shoulder-width apart. With your right hand behind your head and your left hand behind your back, hold a towel between your hands.

- Inhale. Exhale as you bend to the left side. Keep your elbows opened outward. Hold and stretch for 15 seconds, breathing freely. Return to the upright position. Repeat 2 times. Stretch to the other side with the opposite arm position.

Advance by holding and stretching for 25 seconds and bringing your hands closer together on the towel.

7

Waist, Legs • *Hips, Arms, Chest, Shoulders*

• Standing with your feet wide apart, hold a towel between your hands overhead.

• Inhale. Exhale as you bend your left knee and bend to the left side. Allow your right elbow to bend as you pull to the left side with your left arm. Hold and stretch for 15 seconds, breathing freely.

• Return to the upright position. Repeat 2 times. Stretch to the other side.

Advance by holding and stretching for 25 seconds.

8

Achilles' Tendons, Ankles, Thighs, Knees • *Calves, Buttocks, Back, Hips*

• Stand straight, feet shoulder-width apart, arms extended forward.

• Inhale. Exhale as you bend your knees to a squatting position and bend forward with a straight back. Hold and stretch for 15 seconds, breathing freely. Then return to the starting position. Repeat 4 times.

Advance by holding and stretching for 25 seconds and pressing your heels more toward the floor.

9

Legs, Hips • *Calves, Achilles' Tendons, Knees*
• Stand with your feet wide apart.

• Inhale. Exhale as you bend your right knee and gently lunge to the right side. Place your hands on your right knee. Hold and stretch for 15 seconds, breathing freely.

• Stretch to the other side. Repeat 2 times.

Advance by holding and stretching for 20 seconds and deepening the lunge.

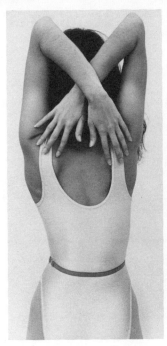

10

Back, Neck, Hamstrings, Buttocks • *Knees, Calves, Arms*

• Stand with your feet shoulder-width apart. Cross your arms behind your head and bend your knees.

• Inhale. Exhale as you bend forward toward your toes. Hang loosely. Hold and stretch for 15 seconds, breathing freely.

• Roll up through each vertebra to stand up. Repeat 4 times.

Advance by holding and stretching for 25 seconds.

STRETCHING OUT   20 minutes

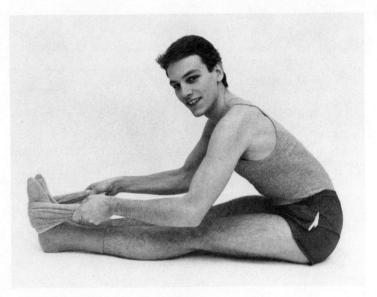

11

Hamstrings, Lower Back • *Calves, Feet, Ankles*

- Sit up straight, legs together, arms at your sides. To stretch your feet and ankles, circle both feet 4 times clockwise, then counterclockwise, flexing and unflexing your toes.

- Flex your feet, aiming your toes toward your head. Drape a towel around your feet.

- Inhale. Exhale as you bend forward from the hips, lowering your torso as close to your legs as possible. Keep your chin lifted and your back straight. Hold and stretch for 20 seconds, breathing freely.

- Relax your legs. Repeat 2 times.

Advance by holding and stretching for 30 seconds.

12

Groin, Hips • *Inner and Outer Thighs, Knees, Back*

• Sitting up straight, put the soles of your feet together and your hands on the insides of your knees.

• Inhale. Exhale as you bend forward from the hips. Keep your lower back straight and your chin lifted. Gently press your knees down. Hold and stretch for 15 seconds, breathing freely.

• Sit up straight again. Repeat 2 times.

Advance by holding and stretching for 25 seconds and moving your feet in closer to you.

13

Inner and Outer Thighs, Hips, Waist • *Groin, Back*

• Sit tall with the soles of your feet together, arms at your sides.

• Inhale. Exhale as you bend forward over your right knee and reach your left arm across. Place your right hand on the floor for support. Hold and stretch for 15 seconds, breathing freely.

• Sit up straight. Repeat 2 times. Stretch to the other side.

Advance by holding and stretching for 25 seconds and reaching across farther.

14

Hips, Waist, Spine, Outer Thighs • *Neck, Buttocks*

• Sitting up straight, cross your right leg over your left, placing your right foot next to the outside of your left calf.

• Twist your upper body to the right, and bring your left arm over your right knee and take hold of your left leg. Put your right hand on the floor behind your torso.

• Inhale. Exhale as you gently push on your left leg with your left arm while twisting your upper body to the right. Look over your right shoulder. Hold and stretch for 15 seconds, breathing freely.

• Relax. Repeat 2 times. Stretch to the other side.

Advance by holding and stretching for 25 seconds.

15

Legs, Groin, • *Hips, Back*

• Sit with your legs a comfortable distance apart.

• Inhale. Exhale as you lean forward from the hips. Extend your arms out in front of you, then put your hands on the floor. Hold and stretch for 20 seconds, breathing freely.

• Walk your hands back to help you return to the upright position. Repeat 2 times.

Advance by holding and stretching for 30 seconds and increasing your reach forward.

16

Hips, Waist • *Legs, Groin, Knees, Arms, Thighs*

- Sitting with your left knee bent so the outside of the knee is on floor, and your right leg straight out to the side, place your hands behind your head.

- Inhale. Exhale as you bend to the right side. Hold and stretch for 20 seconds, breathing freely.

- Return to the upright position. Repeat 2 times. Switch legs and stretch to the other side.

Advance by holding and stretching for 30 seconds and trying to touch the floor with your elbow.

17

Quadriceps, Hamstrings • *Hips, Calves, Achilles' Tendons, Back, Knees*

- Sit up straight with your right leg extended in front and your left knee bent so the inside of the knee is on the floor. Turn your torso to face your right foot. Drape a towel around your right foot.

- Inhale. Exhale as you pull your chest forward toward your right foot. Hold and stretch for 20 seconds, breathing freely.

- Sit up straight again. Repeat 2 times. Stretch to the other side.

Advance by holding and stretching for 30 seconds and lowering your torso closer to your leg.

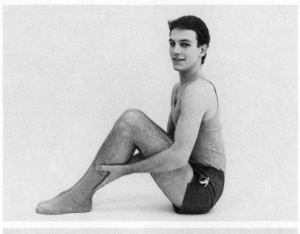

18

Spine, Buttocks • *Hamstrings*

- Sitting, bend your knees toward your chest and put your hands on your calves.

- Inhale. Exhale as you rock back. Hold and stretch for 15 seconds, breathing freely.

- Rock back up to the starting position. Repeat 2 times.

Advance by holding and stretching for 25 seconds and bringing your legs overhead, toes touching the floor.

19

Upper Spine, Neck, Abdominals

• Lying on your back, hands behind your head, bend your knees toward your chest. Keep your feet higher than your knees.

• Inhale. Exhale as you gently pull your head up and forward toward your knees. Hold and stretch for 15 seconds, breathing freely.

• Lower your upper body back down to the floor. Repeat 2 times.

Advance by holding and stretching for 25 seconds.

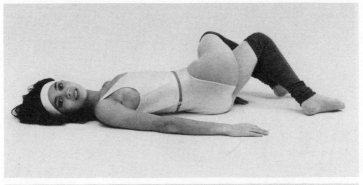

20

Hips, Spine, Abdominals • *Buttocks, Thighs, Waist*

• Lie on your back, knees bent, arms at your sides. Cross your right leg over your left.

• Inhale. Exhale as you pull your right leg toward the left side. Keep your head, upper back, and shoulders on the floor. Hold and stretch for 20 seconds, breathing freely.

• Inhale. Exhale as you pull your right leg toward the right side. Keep your head, upper back, and shoulders on the floor. Hold and stretch for 20 seconds, breathing freely.

• Repeat 1 time. Stretch in the opposite leg position.

Advance by holding and stretching for 30 seconds.

21

Hamstrings, Hips • *Knees, Buttocks*

• Lie on your back with your right leg raised. Bend your left knee and place your left foot on the floor. Holding a towel between your hands, drape it over your right foot.

• Inhale. Exhale as you pull on the towel, moving your right knee toward your chest. Hold and stretch for 15 seconds, breathing freely. Then relax your right leg. Repeat 2 times. Stretch with your left leg.

• Inhale. Exhale as you pull on the towel, moving your right leg—which is now straight—toward your head. Hold and stretch for 15 seconds, breathing freely. Then relax your right leg. Repeat 2 times. Stretch with your left leg.

Advance by holding and stretching for 25 seconds.

22

Hamstrings, Torso • *Hips, Knees*

- Lie on your left side and lean your head into your left hand. Bend your left knee forward for balance and bend your right knee upward. Hold the ends of a towel with your right hand and slip your right foot into the loop.

- Inhale. Exhale as you pull on the towel, moving your right knee toward your right shoulder. Hold and stretch for 15 seconds, breathing freely. Then relax your right leg. Repeat 2 times. Stretch on the other side.

• Inhale. Exhale as you pull on the towel, moving your right leg—which is now straight—toward your head. Hold and stretch for 15 seconds, breathing freely. Then relax your right leg. Repeat 2 times. Stretch on the other side.

Advance by holding and stretching for 25 seconds.

23

Thighs, Buttocks, Hips • *Groin, Hamstrings, Knees, Lower Back*

- Lie on your back with your knees bent toward your chest. Hold a towel between your hands and drape it around your feet.

- Inhale. Exhale as you pull your feet toward your chest and with your elbows gently press your knees open, aiming them to the sides. Hold and stretch for 20 seconds, breathing freely.

- Bring your knees together. Repeat 2 times.

Advance by holding and stretching for 30 seconds.

24

Inner Thighs, Hips • *Legs, Groin, Calves*

• Lie on your back with your legs perpendicular to the floor. Flex your feet back at the ankles.

• Inhale. Exhale as you slowly separate your legs. Place your hands on the insides of your knees and gently press your legs downward. Let gravity help you. Hold and stretch for 20 seconds, breathing freely.

• Bring your legs together. Repeat 2 times.

Advance by holding and stretching for 30 seconds and straightening your knees more fully.

25

Abdominals, Arms, Chest • *Lower Back*

- Lie on your stomach, hands by your shoulders, legs slightly apart.

- Inhale. Exhale as you push down into your hands, lifting your upper body away from the floor. Hold and stretch for 20 seconds, breathing freely.

- Lower your upper body to the floor. Repeat 2 times.

Advance by holding and stretching for 30 seconds.

31

26

Quadriceps, Arms, Shoulders, Chest, Abdominals • *Back*

- Lie face down and bend your knees, aiming your toes toward your buttocks. Hold on to your ankles.

- Inhale. Exhale as you bring your feet closer to your buttocks and press your hips down against the floor. Hold the stretch for 15 seconds, breathing freely.

- Relax. Repeat 2 times.

Advance by holding and stretching for 25 seconds and lifting your chest and knees off the floor. Repeat 2 times.

27

Achilles' Tendons, Ankles, Calves • *Arches, Hamstrings, Buttocks, Arms*

- Stand straight with your feet slightly apart. Bend forward, place your hands on the floor, and walk them forward.

- Inhale. Exhale as you bend your left knee and point your left foot into the floor. Keep your back straight. Hold and stretch for 15 seconds, breathing freely.

- Bend your right knee and point your right foot into the floor. Hold and stretch for 15 seconds, breathing freely.

- Repeat 2 times.

Advance by holding and stretching for 25 seconds and pressing the heel of the rear leg against the floor.

28

Hamstrings, Buttocks, Back, Knees • *Achilles' Tendons, Calves, Shoulders, Arms*

- Kneel on all fours, weight evenly distributed, back flat, fingers pointing forward.

- Inhale. Exhale as you straighten your knees, lifting your buttocks toward the ceiling. Press your heels toward the floor. Hold and stretch for 20 seconds, breathing freely.

- Return to the starting position. Repeat 2 times.

Advance by holding and stretching for 30 seconds and straightening your knees more fully.

29

Quadriceps, Hips • *Knees*

- From a kneeling position, slide your right foot forward so your right knee is directly over your ankle. Put your hands on either side of your right foot.

- Inhale. Exhale as you tilt your pelvis forward and lower the front of your left hip. Hold and stretch for 20 seconds, breathing freely.

• Relax. Repeat 2 times. Stretch in the opposite leg position.

Advance by holding and stretching for 30 seconds and bending your back leg inward to hold that foot with your hand. Repeat 2 times in each leg position.

COOLING DOWN   5-7 minutes

30

Forearms, Wrists

• On all fours, point your fingers toward your knees.

• Inhale. Exhale as you lean back slightly. Hold and stretch for 20 seconds, breathing freely.

• Move your body forward to relax your arms. Repeat 4 times.

Advance by holding and stretching for 30 seconds.

31

Arms, Shoulders • *Back, Chest*

• In a kneeling position, rest your head on your right arm. Extend your left arm forward. Keep your back straight.

• Inhale. Exhale as you reach as far forward as you can with your left hand. Hold and stretch for 20 seconds, breathing freely.

• Relax. Repeat 2 times. Stretch in the opposite arm position.

Advance by holding and stretching for 30 seconds.

32

Arms, Back, Thighs, Buttocks • *Shoulders, Knees*

- Sitting on your heels, rest your chest on your knees and your head on the floor.

- Inhale. Exhale as you reach forward with both arms. Hold and stretch for 20 seconds, breathing freely.

- Relax your arms. Repeat 4 times.

Advance by holding and stretching for 30 seconds.

33

Whole-Body Relaxer

- Sit on your heels and rest your chest on your knees and your head on the floor. Put your arms down at your sides with the palms of your hands facing up. Relax your neck, shoulders, arms, and back. Breathe freely.

- After 30–60 seconds slowly stand up by first rolling onto your side, then putting your feet flat on the floor.

Stretches with Extras

Stretching with extras—a chair, for example—adds another dimension to stretching. And variety as well as a challenge, even in exercise, plays a big part in enjoying and succeeding in whatever you do.

The following stretches with extras can be done before or after the Stretch Out, or any other time.

The chair used for these stretches represents anything that can give you that support: walls, trees, fences, ledges, sinks, refrigerators, desks, cabinets, tables, counters, etc. So no matter where you are, there's always an "extra" that can be utilized for these stretches.

If you use a chair, put the seat firmly against a wall so it doesn't slide around. And be sure not to pull on the chair: if it tipped over, you could fall backward.

STRETCHES
USING A CHAIR   15-20 minutes

1

Hamstring, Buttocks, Back • *Shoulders, Arms*

• Stand about three feet away from the back of a chair, feet wide apart, arms extended forward.

• Inhale. Exhale as you bend forward from the hips until your torso is perpendicular to the floor. Place your hands on the chair. Hold and stretch for 20 seconds, breathing freely.

• Bend your knees as you straighten up to a standing position. Repeat 4 times.

Advance by holding and stretching for 30 seconds and lowering your torso closer to the floor.

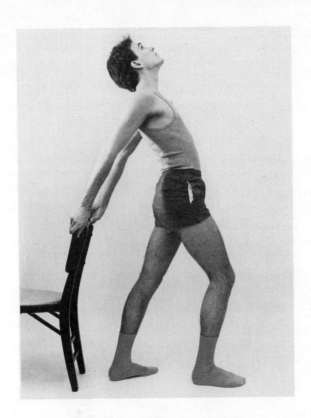

2

Calves, Achilles' Tendons, Chest, Shoulders, Arms • *Knees, Back, Abdominals*

- Stand with your back to a chair an arm's length away. Hold the chair with your hands.

- Inhale. Exhale as you lunge forward with your right leg, bending your right knee. Keep your left leg straight. Lift your chin. Hold and stretch for 15 seconds, breathing freely.

- Bring your legs together again. Repeat 4 times. Lunge with your other leg.

Advance by holding and stretching for 25 seconds.

43

3

Calves, Achilles' Tendons • *Hamstrings*

- Facing a chair about two feet away, with your feet hip-width apart, put your hands on the chair.

- Inhale. Exhale as you lean forward, bending your knees. Gently push your hips forward. Hold and stretch for 20 seconds, breathing freely.

- Stand straight to relax your legs. Repeat 4 times.

Advance by holding and stretching for 30 seconds and pressing your heels against the floor more.

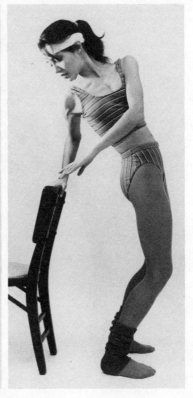

4

Spine, Waist • *Arms, Shoulders, Legs*

- Stand with your back to a chair an arm's length away, feet hip-width apart. Hold the chair with your hands.

- Inhale. Exhale as you bend your knees and reach across to the right side of the chair with your left hand. Twist your upper body to the right but keep your hips facing forward. Hold and stretch for 20 seconds, breathing freely.

- Return to the starting position. Repeat 4 times. Stretch to the other side.

Advance by holding and stretching for 30 seconds.

45

5

Waist, Hips, Arms • *Chest, Shoulders*

• Stand with your right side to a chair an arm's length away. Put your right hand on the chair and cross your left foot past your right.

• Inhale. Exhale as you bend to the right side, reaching your left arm overhead, then to the right. Hold and stretch for 20 seconds, breathing freely.

• Stand upright. Repeat 4 times. Stretch to the other side.

Advance by holding and stretching for 30 seconds and bending farther.

6

Quadriceps, Groin, Hips • *Arms, Back*

• Face a chair an arm's length away. Place your hands on the chair.

• Inhale. Exhale as you slide your left leg back and bend your right knee. Your right knee should be positioned directly over your right ankle. Hold and stretch for 15 seconds, breathing freely.

• Bring your left leg back to your right and stand up. Stretch with your other leg. Repeat 4 times.

Advance by holding and stretching for 25 seconds and pushing the hip of the rear leg farther forward toward the floor.

7

Thighs, Knees • *Hips*

- Facing a chair, with both hands on it, position your feet very wide apart and point them slightly to the outside.

- Inhale. Exhale as you bend your left knee and lunge to the left side. Hold and stretch for 15 seconds, breathing freely.

- Straighten your left knee and return upright. Repeat 4 times. Lunge to the other side.

Advance by holding and stretching for 25 seconds and deepening the lunge.

8

Hips, Thighs, Back, Knees, Buttocks • *Groin, Calves, Achilles' Tendons*

- Face a chair an arm's length away and put your left foot on it. Place your hands on either side of your left foot.

- Inhale. Exhale as you bend your left knee more and lean forward, gently pushing your right hip forward. Keep your back straight. Hold and stretch for 15 seconds, breathing freely.

• Relax. Repeat 4 times. Stretch with your other leg.

Advance by holding and stretching for 25 seconds. Also, straighten your front leg while bending your standing leg and bend forward to lower your torso to your leg. Repeat 4 times in each leg position.

9

Hips, Waist, Knees, Thighs, Hamstrings • *Buttocks, Calves, Achilles' Tendons, Abdominals*

- Stand with your right side to a chair, with your right hand and foot on the chair. Put your right hand in front of your right foot and your left hand on your hip.

- Inhale. Exhale as you bend your right knee more and lean

51

sideways toward the chair. Keep your back straight. Hold and stretch for 15 seconds, breathing freely.

• Straighten up. Repeat 4 times. Stretch to the other side.

Advance by holding and stretching for 25 seconds. Also, straighten your leg on the chair while bending your standing leg and bend sideways toward the chair. Repeat 4 times in each leg position.

Spontaneous Stretching

Stretching is an easy, healthful way to work out the stress that's present in your body so you can alleviate those all-too-frequent nervous, cramped, wound-up feelings, which can lower your energy and performance levels as well as hamper your relationships and health.

So don't overlook any chance to stretch. Help make your body more relaxed and in control; look terrific and feel great. Every day, everywhere.

I've suggested some stretches to do spontaneously, but feel free to add any others from the program.

	Stretch Out Exercise	Stretches with Extras
At the office	2, 3, 4, 8, 9, 10 (in a sitting position)	all
In front of the TV	11, 12, 13, 14, 15, 16, 17, 20, 22	
During telephone conversations, especially waiting time	3, 8	
In the kitchen		all
In the park	all	all

	Stretch Out Exercise	Stretches with Extras
While traveling	2, 3, 4, 10 (in a sitting position)	
After you've been sitting a long time	9, 10	2, 4
After getting out of the car	2, 3	1, 2, 3
Lying down and reading	20 and 24	
To relax before a date or a meeting	2, 3, 10	1
Before going to bed	2, 3, 4, 5, 6, 8, 9 10, 31, 32, 33	1, 5

Here are some stretches that will treat isolated areas prone to minor aches and pains, stiffness, and tension.

Problem	Stretch Out Exercise	Stretches with Extras
For a stiff neck	2, 3, 19	
For an aching back	10, 19, 32, 33	
For leg cramps and stiffness	8, 9, 21, 22, 23, 24 27, 28	1, 2, 8, 9
For shoulder tension	3, 5, 19, 31, 32, 33	2, 5
For tight calves	11, 27, 28	1, 2, 3, 7

Taking 5

Did you know that if you don't cool down after a vigorous exercise session, blood can pool in your legs, causing dizziness, even fainting? And that without a warm-up of stretching your body before undertaking your physical activities, pulled muscles, shin splints, backaches, Achilles' tendonitis from running, and sore shoulders and elbows from tennis are more likely to occur?

That's why it's essential to start and finish any exercise regimen, sport, dance, or running activity by warming up and cooling down your body, especially those specific muscle groups worked in that particular activity.

Follow the warming-up exercises of the Stretch Out for an overall stretch, plus these individual stretches especially selected to warm up, then cool down those areas of your body on which your sport or other physical activity makes the most demands. Except as a cool-down, omit the first exercise of the Stretch Out's warm-up, as it would be too invigorating.

Taking 5 before and after your physical activities will help make whatever you do easier, safer, and more rewarding—and, as a result, much more fun.

Activity	Stretch Out Exercise	Stretches with Extras
Backpacking	28	1, 2
Baseball, softball, basketball, volleyball, football, handball	31	3, 4
Bicycling	14, 21	9
Bowling	13, 27, 31	
Fitness machines	29	1, 4
Golf	20, 22	2
Gymnastics, dancing	24, 25	6
Horseback riding	18, 23	7
Racket sports, including tennis and squash	26, 31	8
Running	11, 27	6
Skating	15, 29	2
Skiing	13, 20, 27	
Soccer	14, 17, 28	
Surfing		1, 4, 6
Swimming	31, 26	2
Weight training	18, 19, 30	